Fix
Yourself
First

New Edition

Fix Yourself First

25 tips to stop ruining your relationships

Kristie Overstreet
Ph.D., LPCC, CST

ISBN 978-0-9979347-4-8 (ebook)

ISBN 978-0-9979347-5-5 (print)

To Rob—you have taught me more about relationships than I ever thought possible. Not a day passes that I'm not grateful to have you in my life. Thank you for not just being my partner but also my best friend.

CONTENTS

ACKNOWLEDGMENTS

To my clients over the past decade, thank you for allowing me to be a part of your relationship journey. You teach me something new every day, and for that I am forever grateful.

To Maria Morao, the incredible illustrator who created the artwork for this book, thank you for your hard work.

To my girlfriends, who have been there with me through the laughter, tears, and heartaches. We always said our stories belonged in a book.

To my parents and sister, thank you for always supporting me in everything I do. Thank you for always telling and showing me that hard work pays off. You've never judged or left me, and for that I'm the luckiest girl in the world.

INTRODUCTION

You may be wondering why I wrote the second edition of *Fix Yourself First* after publishing the first edition last year. I realized I had so much more information to give you that I didn't include in the first edition. As I work with individuals and couples, I learn something new every day. I wanted to include more stories, information, tips, and techniques to help you improve your relationship. I also wanted to include three new quizzes to help you better understand yourself and your relationships. I hope this new information helps you make the changes you need in order to get the relationship you deserve.

The idea for this book came from both my professional and personal experiences with relationships. As many women do, I've stayed past the expiration date in more than one unhealthy relationship, focused on the hope that my partner would change. I spent too much time hoping and wishing and didn't take the time to look in the mirror at what *I* needed to do differently. This led me to the same result in the next relationship.

It was through my personal growth and the amazing experience of working with clients over the past decade that I learned to accept the idea that the changes I needed to make started with me. I had to focus on improving myself versus waiting for my partner to change. Unhealthy partners didn't change, but I could. When I made changes for the better, my tolerance for unhealthy relationships also changed, which gave me the confidence and direction I needed to pursue healthy relationships.

This book is for all gender identities, sexual orientations, and types of relationships. I use the term *partner* throughout this book and in my daily life to be inclusive of all people. I hope you enjoy the tips and techniques I recommend to fix yourself first so you can find the healthiest relationship possible.

TIP 1:
DEAL WITH YOUR CONTROL ISSUES

No one wants to be labeled as having control issues. Women don't begin relationships and think about how they can control things, and most women don't realize they have an issue with needing to be in control. But it is an issue if it's causing a problem in your relationship.

Relationships aren't a one-way street where the focus is only on the needs of one partner. A healthy relationship is one that flows steadily between both partners. The ups and downs are normal and to be expected. If your ups and downs are extreme, you need to evaluate what's causing them. Are there problems with listening or speaking to one another? What patterns are you noticing that lead to conflict?

Think about your expectations for your partner. Take a sheet of paper, think about what you expect from them, and write it out. Don't wait till later. Maybe you expect trust, loyalty, fairness, and/or love. For example, you may expect that your partner always be loyal to you or always meet your needs.

Now, looking back at what you've written, are some of your expectations unrealistic? Are any of them impossible for your partner to provide? Look for words such as *should*, *ought to*, *must*, and *always*. These words create expectations that are often demanding and unrealistic.

How do you define control? How does your partner define control? Your control issues may be choking your relationship. If you think, "This is just who I am," you need to look inward and make changes. If you find another way to justify your need to control things, you need to look at how that's affecting your relationship. Just because you have done something a certain way for so long doesn't mean it is okay to continue doing that thing if it's hurting you or your relationship.

DO YOU HAVE CONTROL ISSUES?

Has your current or a past partner told you that you have control issues? If so, did it make you angry? Is it possible you have issues with needing to control things around you?

As a reminder, something is only considered an issue if it affects you and/or your relationship in a negative way. If you are unsure, try asking your partner or those you are close to. If they feel like you are controlling or have control issues, it's worth taking the time to look inward.

The need to have control comes from within. It is important to explore what this is about, but be gentle with yourself on this journey.

The need for control often comes from a place of fear. You may be afraid of what may happen if things are out of your control. What if things don't go as planned? What if you lose something important to you? What if you get hurt? What if your partner cheats on you? What if they stop liking or loving you?

These worries are real. However, almost all the things we fear will happen actually don't. If it's true that 99 percent of the things we worry about don't come true, maybe you can let go of some of your fears. You are more likely to lose your partner if you continue to be controlling. This will make your fears a reality.

There is a big difference in having things go the way you would like them to and *always* getting your way. There is nothing wrong with wanting to see life happen a certain way. However, if you keep trying to control or attempting to change your partner, you may find yourself alone. You would then be solely responsible for making the fear of losing your partner a reality. No one gets their way most of the time. Why would you be any different? What makes you think things have to go exactly how you want them to?

EXAMPLES OF CONTROL ISSUES

- Excessive calling, texting, or trying to contact your partner throughout the day.
- An obsessive need to know where your partner is at all times.
- Telling your partner how they need to spend their money.
- Not wanting to go out with friends or do things as an individual without your partner.
- Using sex as a reward or punishment.
- Using the silent treatment when you don't like something your partner says or does.

If you choose to continue this type behavior, it will cause your partner to be more defensive, combative, and to emotionally shut down. Have you conditioned your partner to respond in a way that leads to arguing? Do you realize how your behavior is contributing to the issues in the relationship?

THE POWER OF YOUR REACTION

Think about how you react when you don't get your way. Can you roll with it, or do you get angry, pout, and put up a wall?

Though things can't always work to your advantage and you may not be able to control how things turn out, you can always control how you react.

And this is important because your reaction determines the health of your relationship. Your power to change how you handle situations is your best chance of seeing improvement. This doesn't mean you have to respond positively or agree with how things happened, but you have a better chance of getting the outcome you desire if you react in a calm, understanding, and assertive manner.

Avoid overreacting, and think before you speak. Not everything that happens to you or within your relationship requires a reaction from you. If you want your needs met, work on your how you respond. Work smarter, not harder. It takes two healthy people to make a functional relationship, and you are responsible for your half. Stop trying to control the other.

BE THE CHANGE

Dealing with reality and holding yourself accountable is not always easy. But if you want to see any changes in your relationship, you have to be the change. You have to fix yourself first so you can see what's healthy versus what's unhealthy. Don't perpetuate behavior you don't want in your life. Your behavior is the only thing you have control over.

You can't change your partner, regardless of how hard you try. If you have tried it, you'll know it doesn't work. What does work is when you change your behavior, because it affects your partner by allowing them to see the changes you have made, giving them the opportunity to make changes in themselves if they choose to.

If you are struggling with the fact that it's you who needs to change, think about it like this. If you throw a rock in a lake, it creates a ripple effect. The ripple moves through the surface and touches everything around it. The same is true when you accept the need to change. When you change your behaviors and actions, it affects everything around you. There is power in fixing yourself first.

As you get healthier, you will notice that your tolerance for dealing with a dysfunctional partner decreases. The improvements you are making in your life will give you the opportunity to see just how unhealthy your relationship is. If your partner refuses to do their half, you may have to make decisions about the future of your relationship.

HOMEWORK

The following are a few questions and thoughts to get you thinking about how you can change your need for control.

1. When did you start noticing you had control issues?

2. Are your control issues affecting your partner?

3. What are you afraid of in regard to your relationship?

4. Are there any outside influences that led to your fears?

4. What would happen if your fears actually came true?

6. How likely is it that your fears will come true?

7. What can you do to decrease the chance that your fears will come true?

8. Think of a situation involving your need for control. Examine your thoughts and beliefs about the situation. Did you use demand words

such as *always, never, should, shouldn't,* or *must?* Avoid these words and try replacing them with phrases such as *would like to, wish that, it would be better if,* and *it would be nice if.* Demand words keep you stuck in an irrational place and hinder growth. Try to catch yourself if you use them, then do your best to replace them.

9. Be grateful you're not responsible for controlling your partner. If you were, you would also be responsible for their actions. It's hard enough to be responsible for own. Don't try to take on extra work. Focus on what you need to improve and forget the rest.

TIP 2:
STOP THE NEGATIVE SELF-TALK

Have you been around a friend, family member, or partner who is always negative? You try to help them by telling them how great they are, and you remind them that things aren't as bad as they seem, but you end up feeling drained and irritated because no matter what you say, they continue to put themselves down.

Do you remember Eeyore, the beloved donkey from Winnie the Pooh? Though he's cute and loveable, no one can stand to be around him all the time. His negativity and self-deprecation are depressing. It doesn't matter how many times Pooh or Piglet try to boost his morale, he always has something negative to say.

If you have turned into an Eeyore, you've got a problem. If you are constantly putting yourself down and have a difficult time finding something positive to say about yourself, it's time for a change. Only when you take accountability for your misery can you change for the better.

YOU DO AFFECT OTHERS

Your negativity affects the people around you more than you realize. I'm not trying to make you feel worse; I'm trying to help you understand that you need to change whatever it is that's making you unhappy.

You wouldn't want your partner to continue to put themselves down. You know what a turnoff that can be. No one wants to be in a relationship with someone who is constantly saying negative things about themselves.

It's not your partner's job to fix you or make you feel better about yourself. You will not get the validation you think you need from other people. There is no one and nothing that can do this for you. It's your job to repair this, starting from the inside.

FORGET THE WHY

If your parents, family, or ex-partner wreaked havoc on your self-esteem, you already know where some of your issues stem from. The bad news is you can't change the past or what they've said. The good news is that you can change for the better and improve how you see yourself.

Those people and experiences don't define who you are today. They no longer have that power. *You* have the power to define who you are. *You* are the one who can stop ruining your relationship, and it's time to take action.

Be careful to not get stuck in trying to figure out where your negative self-talk comes from. Don't drown in the questions that start with "Why." It doesn't really matter where your self-esteem issue came from. All that matters now is that you commit to repairing them. Stay focused on the solutions and not the causes. It's time to take accountability and to change.

NEGATIVITY CAN SUFFOCATE
YOUR RELATIONSHIP

I worked with Annette and Lyle a few years back. Lyle's complaint was about how Annette said negative things about herself almost on a daily basis. She was fat, she was ugly, and she couldn't understand why Lyle wanted to be with her. For a long time, he countered her comments with positives and reminded her how much he loved her for who she was.

But he soon realized it didn't matter how many times he showered her with praise—she continued with her negative self-talk. That negativity got worse, and Lyle gave up trying to convince her that her negative thoughts were false. Instead, he remained quiet every time she began deprecating herself.

As time passed, Annette's negative attitude became very unattractive to Lyle. Their communication deteriorated, their intimacy changed, and both felt disconnected from one another. During one of their arguments, Annette accused Lyle of not caring about her. She told him she felt he didn't care about her because he'd stopped giving her positive comments. This was the breaking point for Lyle.

He was finally able to tell Annette that he found her attitude and self-talk unattractive. He shared his nervousness over being honest with her because he didn't want to hurt her, and he told her he could not stay in a relationship with someone who was so hard on themselves. He also shared that he'd stopped giving her compliments because she didn't listen and that if she really had listened to him, she would have considered changing how she saw herself.

Lyle's honesty about how he was feeling and how she treated herself had a big impact on Annette. She realized he had actually begun to see her in the negative light she saw herself. This motivated her to start individual counseling, where she was able to see the need to fix how she viewed herself because she owed it to her half of the relationship.

As time passed, Annette was able to change the way she saw herself and to stop her negative self-talk. Her resulting improved sense of confidence had a huge effect on their relationship.

LEARN TO ACCEPT COMPLIMENTS

If you feel you don't deserve compliments or positive things, don't expect to see the changes you are looking for. You'll need to work on receiving the positives and allowing them to fully sink in. As time passes and you continue to improve, you will see the changes come.

For example, when someone gives you a compliment, just say thank you. Do not minimize the compliment, disagree with them, or automatically give them a compliment in return. Just breathe, hold your head up, and thank them. This may feel weird at first, but it gets easier with practice.

Don't think you can feel unworthy and have a healthy relationship at the same time. It is impossible, just as you can't have war and peace at the same time. Don't trick yourself into thinking your relationship is healthy when your self-esteem is not. You can't continue your negative self-talk and expect to be in a relationship with someone who's healthy.

NEGATIVITY ATTRACTS NEGATIVITY

There is enough negativity in the world. Don't add to it and make yourself unattractive with negative self-talk. Remember that what you put out is what you get back. If you send out negativity, you will get it in return. If you constantly put yourself down and see yourself as unworthy, you will attract someone with similar feelings.

Negativity attracts negativity. A healthy person will find your self-talk unattractive and won't stick around for long. As long as you see yourself in a negative light, so will the rest of the world.

WHAT ARE YOU GAINING FROM YOUR BEHAVIOR?

What do you gain from your negative self-talk? Can you identify what that might be? If you weren't hoping to get something in return, you wouldn't keep doing it. One thing you may be hoping for is that someone agree with you, though that may not be something you realize as a conscious thought.

Do you find your close friends do the same thing? Do they talk negative and put themselves down? Misery loves company.

Maybe you hope that someone won't agree with you, that maybe they will tell you how silly you are for thinking about yourself in such a negative light. Whatever you are seeking to gain from this behavior, it is dysfunctional. Now is the time to assess, question, and change that behavior. You are the only one who's responsible for the way you see yourself. The goal is to shine out positivity. If you do, it's more likely you will get it back. If you want a positive and confident partner, be one. It isn't magic. It is simply putting out what you want to get back. If you can't motivate yourself to make the change, think back to Eeyore and remind yourself that there is nothing attractive about being a downer.

HOMEWORK

Here are a few assignments to help improve your self-talk.

1. Have an honest conversation with yourself. Write out the answers to these questions: Are you really as bad as you think or say you are? Are you so negative you have to constantly remind yourself and others of it? What have you done that makes you see yourself in a negative light? What evidence do you have that you are unworthy?

2. Make a list of fifty positive things about yourself. Come up with twenty-five things and then ask the people in your life to give you an

additional twenty-five. No repeats! Do not worry that you're being narcissistic or full of yourself. Give yourself permission to complete this exercise of improving your self-esteem. After you identify your fifty positive things, post them where you can see them every day. You'll be reminded of how awesome you are and how you have the ability to believe positive things about yourself. You are not as bad as you thought you were.

3. Get accountable and ask to be called out. Take a personal challenge and ask your friends to call you out if you say something negative about yourself. This will bring it to your attention and give you the opportunity to change your behavior. Every time you catch yourself, or your friends catch you saying something negative, counter it with something positive. It will feel weird at first, but once you start, it will get easier. You can do this!

TIP 3:
KNOW WHEN TO TALK AND
WHEN TO LISTEN

Timing is everything when it comes to communicating with your partner. There is a time to talk and a time to listen. Don't feel like this applies to you?

Well, it's unrealistic to think you should be able to talk about anything and everything you want at any given time. Relationships don't work that way. This doesn't mean you can't communicate how you want to. It does mean you need to be aware of when to talk and when to listen. This has nothing to do with being a woman and everything to do with getting your needs met.

LISTENING IS AN ACTION

The term *listening* is a verb, an action word. Imagine what you could learn about your partner's needs if you stopped talking and started listening. The key to getting your needs met lies in being in tune with what your partner needs.

Showing love by listening to your partner is a great way to model how you would like your partner to listen to you. It also gives you the opportunity to talk about your needs and helps you learn specifically when to speak up so you get those needs met.

It's a give and take. When we argue and each partner feels like they are right, we become defensive, past hurts are revisited, and we dig our heels in and refuse to back down, effectively throwing up a roadblock, where no one is listening or communicating effectively.

When we don't have the tools we need to resolve an argument, it leads to a cycle where the real issues that need to be resolved become buried and the relationship becomes more strained. Resentment toward one another quickly builds, and many are unable to break out of this cycle without professional help.

DIFFERENCES IN COMMUNICATION

There are definitely differences in how men and women communicate. Women typically have their "word bag" full about 95 percent of the time. This means women almost always have something to say.

Your partner may have something to say, but you may not be aware of it. It's not because you don't want to hear them. In most cases women want their partner to talk more. But if you are talking all the time, when will your partner be able to speak up?

As females, we are wired to talk, but wired or not, we need to control when we talk and when we listen if we want to build a healthy relationship with our partner.

I'm sure it doesn't surprise you that men are wired differently. Men typically talk only to extract information in order to solve a problem. Women talk and vent to problem solve. Talking things out helps them process and figure out issues.

When women talk, men take in all of their words and process everything from a problem-solving perspective. But when there are too many details at one time, men shut down like machines that get overheated.

This often leads men to jump in and interrupt women by offering a solution, which in turn infuriates women, who are still explaining the details and have not asked for a solution. Men often feel that women won't stop talking or can't get to their point fast enough. They don't want to be bothered by the details. What is a woman to do, then, if she needs a man to listen to her talk through her problems?

TEACH THEM TO LISTEN

You can help your partner to be a better listener. When you want to talk about something, tell them you need them to only listen. Let them know you don't need a solution or advice. This helps them understand what you need in the moment.

Also, you want to be sure they have time to listen to you. If it isn't a good time, don't take it personally or react negatively. If they don't have time, they may interrupt or not be fully present.

Your ability to tell your partner you need them to listen allows them to be there for you. It allows them to sit back and be present in the moment and gives them the opportunity to turn off the problem-solving mentality. If you do need their help with a problem, let them know you are open to their suggestions—but only after you're finished talking.

Jane and Dale are a good example of this. Jane wants to talk to Dale about her frustrations with a coworker. She wants to figure out the best way to handle the situation. She makes sure Dale is available to listen by asking him if he has a few minutes to talk. When he says yes, she tells him she needs him to simply let her talk it out without offering any solutions.

Jane has freed Dale from having to find a solution. Since Dale is a natural problem solver, it is helpful for Jane to tell him what she needs from him. He is able to sit back and be present so she can vent and figure out how to handle the issue with her coworker. Because she's made her needs clear, it is unlikely Dale will jump in and interrupt her. This would have happened if she didn't tell him what she needed prior to talking. You may not be able to do this every time, but the goal is to do it as often as possible.

BE A GOOD LISTENER

It is also important to be a good listener when your partner needs to talk. Be present and don't jump in and interrupt with advice or a solution unless they ask for one. Remember that just because they are talking about a situation doesn't mean they want your opinion on it. If you are unsure, ask if they want you to share your thoughts or if they just need you to listen.

And remember that not every problem or issue needs to be talked out. You don't need to share everything you are feeling all the time with your partner. Make sure you have other healthy, trustworthy outlets, such as friends and/or family. Also, be sure you make time for exercise, hobbies, interests, and anything that can help you work through issues.

Don't take it personally if your partner isn't interested in every detail of your life. This is one of the many benefits of having friends you can vent to. Don't make the mistake of taking everything to your partner, or you will end up being disappointed and not getting your needs met. Your partner can't be everything for you.

LITTLE THINGS CAN TURN INTO BIG THINGS

Sadly, many women have lost touch with the unspoken acts of affection that indicate they are present with their partner. These include things like sitting next to one another on the couch, a nightly ritual, and kissing their partner before leaving the house. These small but vital demonstrations of affection help reassure each partner that everything is okay.

We tend to take these simple gestures for granted until they stop happening. Interestingly, they are the first sign that there are issues with the relationship. Their absence is a red flag that the relationship needs immediate attention because these little things turns into big things. If you want a healthy relationship, you'll need to stop neglecting your partner and holding back affection. If your partner is the one holding back, let them know how much you miss their little attentions. Make sure you are doing these things daily and tell your partner how much you enjoy it when he does them.

HOMEWORK

The following exercises will help you explore your needs, examine your listening skills, and better connect with your partner.

1. Answer yes or no to the following questions: Do you not know what you need so you stay quiet? Do you think you do not have any needs? Do you know what your needs are and hope that your partner will figure them out? Do you know what your needs are and tell your partner but they still don't get met?

2. Even though women typically like to problem solve by talking things out, they sometimes don't realize that not every problem or situation needs to be talked out with their partner. Your partner's problem-solving process may be totally different than yours. The goal is to work on seeing things from their perspective. Have you asked them how they like to solve problems? Have you tried to connect with them in their process? If not, give it a try. Worst case, your empathy and understanding of their process will have increased, which can only help the two of you connect in a more intimate way.

3. Explore how you currently use unspoken acts of affection to communicate. Have you neglected these acts in your relationship? When was the last time you initiated a hug or kiss? Have you showed gratitude to your partner in the last twenty-four hours? Your partner may respond by meeting your needs if you are reaching out to them in a genuine way.

TIP 4:
GIVE COMPLIMENTS AND
EXPRESS GRATITUDE DAILY

Don't assume that just because a couple has been together for years they are happy and in love. This is the case for some but not for the majority. Most couples who have been together for a long time do love one another. However, the concept of being in love isn't enough to keep two people happy or sustain a relationship. Love is just a word unless it's accompanied by action, and for a couple to be truly happy and healthy, this action is required on a regular basis.

One of the most understated but important acts of love is giving a compliment or expressing gratitude every day. Have you or your partner gotten out of the habit of saying something positive to each other or of being grateful for one another? If so, you need to make changes immediately.

Don't slip into the victim role by thinking that your partner should be the one doing this for you. You are the one who needs to take action. It's truly the only way to see your partner make changes. You have to be the change.

DON'T GET STUCK IN A CYCLE

Cheryl and Natasha came to see me a few years ago because they couldn't stop arguing. I was amazed how each had a sarcastic comeback every time one of them brought up an issue. It was obvious they were stuck in a cycle of hurt and pain. They couldn't figure a way out, so they continued tearing one another to pieces.

I remember asking them in their first session when they'd last told one another thank you or given each other a compliment. They looked at me and then turned toward one another, a little stunned. I could tell neither had realized until that moment that they had been neglecting this part of their relationship. A few seconds passed before they again began pointing the finger at each other, accusing the other of not saying thank you. Just as quickly as they'd realized their deficit, they'd fallen right back into their cycle of defensiveness.

I let them go at it a few more minutes before they stopped talking and looked at me. When they noticed me smiling, they smiled and looked at one another again, suddenly realizing that the only thing they could agree on was that the other one was the problem. They were then able to see that their tendency to blame and lack of personal accountability were reinforcing their cycle of arguing.

It was at this point they were ready to work. They were able to identify what they were grateful for about each other and even began giving small compliments during the session. Through mirroring and listening, they began to reconnect. As they practiced their new skills at home, it didn't take long before they'd created a new habit of giving compliments and expressing gratitude on a daily basis, which enabled them to connect better than ever before and feel appreciated within the relationship.

SELF-REFLECTION

If you can't remember the last time you complimented or expressed your gratitude to your partner, do it now. Literally stop reading this book and call or text a compliment to your partner.

You only have today and are not promised tomorrow. Imagine if you were to wake up tomorrow and your partner had passed away. Would you have done things differently? Will it require you to lose your partner to make you see the need to change your behavior?

What if you feel resentful or unappreciated? Can you still put forth the effort? How do you know your partner doesn't feel the same way? Try to identify your resentments, work through them, and start appreciating what you have.

A compliment can be as simple as saying thank you for making the coffee this morning. There's power in gratitude. Even if you're in a negative space within your relationship, you can begin to bridge your differences by speaking up and offering a compliment or expressing gratitude. You can be the change.

THE POWER OF VULNERABILITY

Are you struggling to give compliments because it will make you feel vulnerable? If you have had any trust issues within the relationship, you may not want your partner to think that everything is okay just because you gave them a compliment. You may not want your partner to think they are forgiven for what they did and that you are over the issue that caused the breach of trust. It is completely normal to want to protect yourself when you've been hurt.

But your ability to be vulnerable and to let your walls down and say something nice shows just how healthy you are. It's how you can stop the cycle of arguing you're trapped in. You can't wait for the other person to change. *You* have the power to change. You can find something nice to say. If you can't, the relationship is probably near its end. It's your responsibility to find the compliment and to express gratitude to your partner. It's also the best way to increase the chances that you'll receive one in return.

Men typically want to provide and protect those they care about. Women typically want to nurture and support those they care about. The goal is for you to begin to understand these innate characteristics, which can serve as a reminder of what you are grateful for within your relationship. Though you can't expect your partner to be perfect and meet all your expectations, there is probably something they've done for you and your relationship you can be grateful for. Everyone likes to hear compliments. Give out what you want to get in return.

HOMEWORK

This exercise will help you identify compliments and things to be grateful for in your relationship.

1. Make a list of positive things about your partner.

2. Make a list of positive things about your relationship.

3. Make a list of the things you are grateful for about your partner.

TIP 5:
STOP USING WORDS THAT DON'T WORK

Wouldn't it be lovely if you were able to figure out how to work smarter in every area of your life? Well, anything you can do to make sure the relationship is as easy as possible and that your needs met should be your focus. One way to make things easier is to stop using words that aren't helpful.

Did you know that certain words cause arguments? If your goal is to make life easier for yourself, be sure to choose your words wisely. Don't get stuck thinking what if you make changes and your partner does not. In time, if you have made an effort to improve and your partner hasn't, you may have to make a decision about the relationship.

THEY CAN'T READ YOUR MIND

Using the right words to help your relationship is crucial if you want to see change. It's important to remember that your partner cannot read your mind, regardless of how many times you have told them what you like, want, or desire. Be sure to use effective language, or words that have the most power.

Stop and think before you talk and allow yourself a few moments to choose the most effective words in order to get your needs met. Don't worry if you mess up and say the wrong thing. You can ask for a do-over and restate your needs. No one is perfect, so cut yourself some slack.

DEMAND WORDS DON'T WORK

Start by looking at your thoughts and beliefs about the situation you are struggling with. Are you using demand words like *always, never, should, shouldn't*, and *must*? If so, try using words such as *would like to, wish that, it would be better if*, and *it would be nice if* instead

You will find that changing these demand words to more effective phrases immediately decreases your partner's defensiveness. If you use rational words versus irrational demands, you'll greatly improve communication.

One of the most popular demand words we use is *should*. Each of the following *should* statements is ineffective because it is a demand and won't lead to a resolution:

- He should not bring up the past.
- He should have known I would be mad.
- She should ask me if I need help.
- She should tell me if I hurt her feelings.

These phrases are more effective:

- It would be nice if he stopped bringing up the past.
- It would be nice if he could read my mind, but he can't.
- I really wish she would ask me if I needed help.
- It would be great if she told me I hurt her feelings.

It may be difficult at first, but once you start, it will get easier. As you make these changes, you are modeling the kind of change you want to see in your partner. If they see you changing your demand words, it's likely they'll do the same.

WORDS CAN HURT

In working with couples, I often spend a lot of time helping them change their demand statements. Amy and Lisa are a great example of how demand words can hurt a relationship. The couple ended up in my office because they were struggling to connect and were unsure if their relationship would work.

Lisa's favorite word was *always* when describing almost anything Amy did. Amy always did this or that. Amy always had a bad attitude and always acted like a victim. This made Amy feel like she couldn't ever do anything right and kept her from connecting with Lisa. In our work, Amy was able to tell Lisa that this bothered her and made her pull away.

Over time, Lisa became open to feedback and was able to change her demand statements, which led Amy to reconnect with her. Lisa began to catch herself when she said *always* and learned how to rephrase her statements, and the two were able to more effectively listen and communicate with one another. This in turn led to an improved sense of trust within the relationship and a better connection.

Amy and Lisa's difficulty with demand words is a common problem for couples. It usually begins when one or both partners is frustrated because they don't feel heard. This is why it's important to clearly communicate what you need and to get to the root of the issue and not get stuck in the superficial content.

IT'S YOUR RESPONSIBILITY

If you are like the majority of the population, you were not taught how to use effective words. As an adult, it is your responsibility to work smarter, not harder. Don't wait for your partner to change. That may not ever happen. You have to be the change by using words that work.

HOMEWORK

1. Write the following words on a sheet of paper and then tape them to your refrigerator: *should, shouldn't, always, never, must,* and *ought to.* These are the words you want to avoid because they are ineffective. If you continue to use these demand words, you will not see the change you desire.

2. The goal is to catch yourself if you use these words and replace them with the following: *wish that, would be nice if, would be great if, would like to.*

TIP 6:
STOP ACTING LIKE A VICTIM

If you continue to blame others for your issues and problems, you are acting like a child. I'm not minimizing what you have been through, the trauma you have experienced, or the hurt you have endured, but if you want to fix yourself and improve your life, *you* need to heal your hurt.

Bad things happen. You may not be able to forget something that happened to you, but you can heal from it through support, therapy, self-care, or however you choose to.

THE PROBLEM WITH BEING A VICTIM

If you choose to remain in the role of a victim, you sacrifice your opportunity to grow. Victimization keeps you stuck and does not allow room for improvement.

Here are a few examples of what a victim mentality looks like:

- Using the way you grew up as an excuse for why you act the way you do as an adult.
- Unloading your past relationship baggage onto your current relationship.
- Projecting your mommy and/or daddy issues onto your current relationship.
- Blaming your partner and not taking accountability for your actions.
- Having the mindset that it's always someone else's fault and not taking accountability for your actions.

Playing the role of a victim is a full-time job. It takes a vast amount of energy and time to remain stuck there and rents a lot of space in your head. It's time to get rid of a belief system where there are limits that inhibit personal growth. Your life isn't determined without your say. *Your* actions and decisions today determine your tomorrow. *You* have the power and ability to achieve whatever you desire, but you have to do more than just believe it. You have to be willing to make it happen.

DON'T STAY STUCK

If you are acting like a victim, you are not healing, and if you are not healing, you are stuck. And remaining stuck will suck the life out of you. Not to mention it's a major turnoff to your partner. Do you feel the need to drag your partner down with you? Stop throwing a pity party for yourself. You deserve more from life, but you won't get it unless you get out of the victim role.

Maintaining a victim mentality can lead you to build resentment toward your partner. You may think this is what they deserve and that you have a right to do this. But this mentality will keep you in an unhealthy cycle where you continue to experience hurt. Once resentment has begun to build, it can feel almost impossible to overcome.

If you want to feel valued, appreciated, and loved, start with yourself. As time passes, if you don't get love back from your partner, you may need to make other plans for your future.

EMPTY THREATS CAN MAKE YOU FEEL WORSE

Often, when we begin to feel like a victim, we find ourselves making threats against our partner to get what we want. For example, if you find out your partner spoke to an ex, you may naturally feel upset and angry. From a place of fear, you may threaten to leave them if it happens again. With the passage of time, you begin to heal, but when you find out they spoke to their ex again, your immediate response is to get angry and tell them this is their last chance.

This is an example of an empty threat. These threats do not work. They only make you feel worse if you don't follow up on them. If you are going to make a threat, be prepared to follow through with it. If you don't, it has no weight and is useless.

You have the right to leave the relationship at any time; just don't use leaving as a threat. No one is making you stay in an unhealthy relationship. Many clients I work with will threaten to leave the other person. But if this threat is not followed with action, it leads to further resentment that can be almost impossible to heal.

It is your responsibility, and yours alone, to fix yourself. And your changing the things you are responsible for is the best shot you have at improving the relationship.

HOMEWORK

1. Make a victim list. Write down everything you feel has been done wrong to you, happened to you, hurt you, and any actions you blame others for.

2. On a separate sheet of paper, make three categories: Caused by My Partner, Caused by My Family, and Caused by Others. Then take your victim list and put each item in the proper category.

3. Focus on each category and answer these questions: Can I change any of these things? Are there any I can begin to heal from? Which category hurts the most? What is it about this category that hurts the most?

TIP 7:
BE ACCOUNTABLE WHEN
YOU SCREW UP

Accepting responsibility for your actions can be one of the hardest things you'll ever do. Apologizing and admitting you are at fault can leave you feeling vulnerable, especially in an unhealthy relationship.

Being vulnerable means your defenses are down and there is potential for you to be hurt by your partner. You don't want to be the one who caused the problem. It's easier to blame your partner, but if you do, you remain in an unhealthy place.

When you hold yourself accountable and apologize when it is your fault, you are working to fix the problem. Remember to always work to find a resolution; don't add to the problem by placing blame on your partner.

ACCOUNTABILITY LOOKS LIKE THIS

Contemplate the following two examples of accountability:

Example 1: After yelling at your partner, you stop and say, "I'm sorry I just dumped on you. It was me, not you. I messed up. I didn't mean to come off like that. I'm just really frustrated because I don't feel like anything is going right."

Example 2: You come home frustrated and irritable. You find yourself being short with your partner, and you have a bad attitude. You say, "It's not you, it's me, and I'm in a bad mood because my day has been crappy, but I don't need to take it out on you."

Both examples show courage because you're holding yourself accountable and exposing your vulnerability. It can be hard to apologize. But regardless of how difficult it may be, it's the right thing to do, and your partner will thank you. If they don't, that is their issue. You are responsible for your actions only, not theirs. But remember, actions speak louder than words, so don't repeat the behavior you've apologized for.

KNOW YOUR DEFENSE MECHANISMS

There are times in your relationship when you may feel the need to defend yourself. This is when your defense mechanisms can surface. Defense mechanisms are the automatic responses you use to protect yourself. Most of the time these are subconscious and you don't even realize you are using them, but the goal with each is to defend and protect. A few examples of the defense mechanisms we employ are all-or-nothing thinking, overgeneralizing, mind reading, projection, and denial.

If you don't take accountability when you screw up, your relationship will not improve. There is an extreme amount of power in saying "I'm sorry." Give it a try. You may be surprised at the impact it has on your partner.

You *can* change this self-defeating behavior. When you stop blaming others and take full accountability for your actions, you will see a change in your life, and you may find that your partner starts taking accountability for what they do as well. You will also see trust and connection improve as accountability increases.

JUST SAY YOU'RE SORRY

Patrick and Bethany's relationship was a roller coaster from the start. They met, dated, and moved in with each another within two months. They were madly in love, and both were impulsive, so they thought they were a perfect match. Six months into their relationship they decided to seek couples therapy, specifically to work on their communication issues.

After the second session, I noticed that the majority of Patrick's complaints were that Bethany rarely apologized when she was wrong. He stated how unfair he felt it was that he was accountable and she was not. Each time he shared this, Bethany became angry and cited examples of how Patrick had hurt her.

With a little help, she began to realize she was scared to be vulnerable with Patrick. She figured out that it was hard for her to apologize because she was fearful of appearing weak and being hurt again. When she saw the look on his face after she apologized for how she'd acted, she realized the role she'd played in their argument cycle. She also came to realize that when she genuinely apologized for her actions, they argued less. Patrick had his work to do as well, but Bethany was able to change this area of her life, which led to an improvement in their communication.

YOU ARE RESPONSIBLE ONLY FOR YOURSELF

Remember, if your partner doesn't take accountability when they need to, it's not yours to own or fix. You're only accountable for yourself. Though you have no control over your partner, a lack of accountability on their part may cause you to reevaluate your future together.

Who cares at this point in your life if you watched your parents blame one another for their issues? You are not your parents, and it's time to stop living in fear that you're going to be just like them. Be an adult, take accountability when you screw up, apologize, and trust that your partner will do the same.

HOMEWORK

1. Learn to say you are sorry. Identify at least one thing in your relationship you can apologize for no matter how small you think it is. Go to your partner, be accountable, and apologize that you didn't do it sooner.

2. Make an accountability list. Make a list of everything you could have taken accountability for in the past. You don't have to share this list with anyone. It is for your personal growth. Once you have completed your list, look through it and ask yourself if there are any areas you can take accountability for now, in this moment. Then get to work on apologizing or making amends. The goal of this exercise is to help you feel whole and in control of your life. This is a huge step in your growth, so give yourself credit.

TIP 8:
LEARN TO SAY NO AND
TO STOP PEOPLE PLEASING

Do you find it difficult to say no? Do you struggle with people pleasing? What if you were able to say no to those who make unreasonable demands on your time? Many people have this issue and either don't realize it or don't know how to change it. But the inability to say no can affect both you and your relationship.

The struggle to say no often comes from a desire to please others. It may not be obvious that this is happening, and so it's important to figure out what leads us to say yes as often as we do. Maybe we view ourselves as a nice person and think that if we say no, others will view us differently. Maybe we want to help as many people as we can, so we say yes to everything. If you struggle to say no, consider making a change today. If you do not make these needed changes in your life, both you and your relationship will suffer.

EXAMPLES OF WHAT NOT TO DO

If any of these examples sounds familiar, take note. You need to avoid these types of scenarios at all costs.

- You say yes to almost everything your partner asks of you, even when you want to say no. You don't want to cause an argument or make your partner angry. This is how you avoid conflict
- Your family invites you to all of their activities and events. You feel obligated to say yes, even when you want to say no. You try to avoid making anyone upset. You find it easier to go along with them rather than speak up and cause a potential conflict.
- At work, you find it difficult to say no to coworkers. You worry that if you do, they will think negatively of you. You don't want them to think you're not a team player.
- You have a difficult time saying no to a friend who makes demands on your time. She is a good friend, and you assume you will hurt her feelings if you say no. You know she tells you no when she wants to, but you feel as if you can't do the same.

DON'T MAKE YOURSELF MISERABLE

Your struggle to say no may come from a place of wanting to be helpful. It may also come from a place of fear: What will they think if I say no? What if they think I am mean or selfish? What if they think I don't love them or care about them? These thoughts can lead to fear and anxiety. You may even begin to feel resentment and frustration toward those asking favors of you.

This resentment and frustration can spread into other areas of your life and leave you feeling miserable. Your partner may begin to feel that you take on too many things and don't make enough time for them. They may think you say yes to everyone else. Then your relationship suffers, and you have no one to blame but yourself.

The word *no* is one of the first words you learned as a child. We are told no so many times you would think it would be easy to say as an adult. You have every right to say no at any time, but it is your responsibility to speak up for your needs and desires. Your ability to establish boundaries is a gauge for how healthy or unhealthy you are.

JUST SAY NO

I have found that many women who struggle to say no are hard on themselves. Rena is a perfect example. Rena reached out to me because she was struggling with anxiety that affected every aspect of her life. She told me she felt stressed all day, every day. In her many obligations at work and in caring for her parents and young daughter, she *always* said yes when someone asked her for help. She didn't want to be viewed as selfish or mean.

I could hear her frustration as she described her relationships with family and friends. She took care of everyone except herself. I asked her how long she could keep going at her current rate and at the level of anxiety she was experiencing. I also asked her if she would want her daughter doing the same thing as an adult. She instantly said she would never let her daughter act the same way. This was when she realized she had to change.

We discussed how she would view herself if she said no to her family or friends, and we explored her unrealistic expectations. She began to take responsibility for speaking up for her needs and found the courage to say no. Through role-playing and cognitive behavioral therapy (CBT), she was able to say no more often, reduce her anxiety, improve her self-care, and find pride in her ability to be a healthy role model for her daughter.

DON'T WASTE YOUR TIME FIGURING OUT WHY

Don't get lost in trying to figure out why you struggle to say no. Instead, use your energy to recognize when you struggle with the behavior, and start to change it. The world will not crumble, and no one will think you are a horrible person. Do what you need to do for you. If you don't, you have no one to blame but yourself.

HOMEWORK

1. In order to change your people-pleasing tendencies, you'll need to identify your thoughts and beliefs when in specific situations. When you start worrying about what someone will think, immediately say aloud, "So what?" So what if they think you are mean or selfish?

2. You assume that's what they are thinking. If they said no to you, would you think the same thing? You probably wouldn't see it as a big deal coming from them, but since it's from you, it's different. Being your own worst critic can leave you feeling drained.

3. Your role as a people pleaser can leave you feeling empty because you have nothing left to fill yourself up with. This leaves you unable to contribute your half to the relationship. How can you be healthy enough to give your half if you have nothing to give?

4. Don't take it for granted that your partner will always be there. Realize that your relationship and your partner can change at any time. Take back your power, say no when you want to, and get your life back. How many times can you challenge your need to people please today?

TIP 9:
SET HEALTHY BOUNDARIES

Were you taught how to create and maintain personal boundaries? Growing up, who showed you how? Did you see a parent or family member set healthy boundaries? When did you first realize you needed to establish better boundaries? Do you know what your boundaries are?

It's never too late to learn how to establish boundaries. If you avoid this, you will continue to experience unhealthy relationships, friendships, and family conflicts.

WHAT ARE BOUNDARIES?

Boundaries are limits you create for yourself in regard to the people in your life. These limits show others how you want to be treated. Boundaries also show others how you do not want to be treated. If you don't set healthy boundaries, you are susceptible to being treated in an unhealthy way.

When you were growing up, you learned from watching the adults in your life. You subconsciously began to create a mental template of what you were supposed and not supposed to do. Most people are not taught how to establish and maintain good boundaries.

A codependent relationship is one example of not having boundaries. If your feelings, beliefs, and needs are dependent upon your partner's, you may be codependent. If you are worried about how your partner may react to what you want or feel, you need to work on setting boundaries. When you don't give yourself the opportunity to express your preferences, you create an unhealthy relationship.

Give yourself permission to be an individual within the relationship. It's great that you want your partner to be happy, but you can't sacrifice your needs and desires to create this happiness for them. If you do, you will find yourself in chaos and in crazy-making situations where you can't figure out how to end the dysfunction but you can't imagine life without your partner, either.

You have to be able to speak up for what you need. You have to let your partner know what you are okay with and what you are not okay with. If you don't, you will not be able to lead a truly authentic, happy life.

WHAT ARE YOUR PERSONAL BOUNDARIES?

Think about what messages your boundaries say about you and, more importantly, how you expect to be treated. What are you not okay with? What does a boundary mean to you? Here are a few examples of healthy boundaries:

- I am an individual within a relationship and am not codependent.
- I don't allow others to abuse or mistreat me.
- I will end a relationship that isn't mutually beneficial.
- I will leave partners who are self-centered and only care about themselves.
- I will end a relationship where I care more about my partner's needs than my own.

- I refuse to stay in an unhealthy relationship just because I think my partner will change.

Setting a boundary can be as simple as saying no to something you don't want to do. It can also be when you refuse to allow yourself to be treated a certain way. Sometimes setting a boundary looks like ending a relationship that is hurting you.

Our bodies are designed to set boundaries. For example, if you are outside and you feel like you're getting sunburned, you react to protect your skin. Your skin can't continue to burn without pain, which pain then signals your brain to protect your skin. The sunburn demands to be treated by leading you to cover up with protective clothing or by going indoors. If you don't react, the pain will become worse. Your body is telling you to set a boundary, which is to stay out of the sun. Take note from how your body works to keep itself healthy by maintaining certain boundaries.

YOU ARE RESPONSIBLE FOR YOUR BOUNDARIES

You get to decide when you are ready to set boundaries so you can grow as a person. If you are ready to make changes for the better, get started now. Start by defining what boundaries you need to create in your relationships.

To define your boundaries, first decide what you need to speak up about or what behavior you can no longer tolerate in your partner. Second, establish your boundaries so your partner has a clear understanding of your needs. Third, maintain these boundaries. This can be difficult at times because it means being assertive and strong.

Some relationships end when one partner sets healthy boundaries because the other partner won't respect those boundaries. Your best chance of being in a healthy relationship is to define, establish, and maintain your boundaries.

HOMEWORK

1. Define your boundaries by writing them out. Ask yourself which boundaries will help you enjoy a healthy relationship.

2. Establish your boundaries from this list. Ask yourself, "How will I establish each of these boundaries within my relationship?"

3. Maintain your boundaries going forward. Ask yourself, "What will I do to ensure these boundaries remain in place?"

TIP 10:
BE HEALTHY SO YOU CAN
GIVE YOUR 50 PERCENT

If you choose to focus only on what your partner needs to change versus what you need to change, you are avoiding your responsibility within the relationship. Your goal is to fix yourself so you can be as healthy as possible in your half of the relationship.

Hopefully, when your partner sees the changes you are making and the positive effect it's having on your relationship, it will motivate them to take the lead in making changes within themselves. If they do not, at least you will be in healthier space to make the difficult decisions you may have to make.

KEEP YOURSELF HEALTHY FIRST

Do you feel like there just aren't enough hours in the day? Are you so busy taking care of everyone else in your life you don't have time for yourself? Everyone is time poor, so you can no longer use this as an excuse to avoid self-improvement. Your relationship deserves better, and, more importantly, you deserve better.

What are you actively doing to stay healthy? Are you making time for yourself? Do you have an interest or hobby you enjoy? Think about the activities you enjoyed when life wasn't so hectic. Did you enjoy reading, drawing, or working out? If so, begin to think about what small steps you can take to bring the things you enjoy back into your life. If you don't take time for yourself, you will negatively affect your relationship.

STOP AVOIDING SELF-CARE

Lillian is a great example of how easy it is to avoid self-care. Lillian sought counseling because she was frustrated and close to giving up on her relationship. She shared with me her hope that her partner would change in how he communicated and connected with her.

Their relationship was near perfect for the first year, then he changed jobs and she got a promotion. She was thrilled about the promotion, but it almost doubled her work hours and drastically cut her time at home. She told me that when she arrived home at the end of the day, she found herself exhausted and only interested in zoning out in front of the TV. She and her partner began to spend less and less time together. She missed being with him but could barely keep up with her job, much less her relationship.

I asked Lillian to identify the areas of her life that were important to her. These included her relationship, her job, her family, and her friends. After I encouraged her to look at herself as a whole, she added her health and her hobbies. She began to see she wanted her partner to change so he would be more supportive of her long work hours.

Once she realized that her frustration and sadness were because *she* was out of balance, she worked hard to focus on what she had the ability to change, including setting healthy boundaries at work, which meant going in earlier and leaving on time several days a week. She and her partner also picked one night each week to go out on a date. They also set a goal of walking together a few nights a week after dinner.

Once Lillian identified that she was responsible only for her half of the relationship, she was able to focus on herself and establish a new routine that led her to finding a healthy balance. She was able to resolve her frustrations, stop blaming her partner, and feel a sense of accomplishment in her ability to change these areas of her life.

NO ONE EXPECTS YOU TO BE PERFECT

If you've chosen to be in a relationship, you owe it to your partner to function at your *best*, but achieving *perfection* is not the same thing. Often this perfectionist thinking turns into self-sabotage because it's impossible to maintain. The goal is to be healthy more often than not. You want to be better, and you deserve to be better.

A healthy woman is one who is independent, knows what she needs, and works to get her needs met. It's a combination of being able to meet your own needs as well as share these needs with your partner. If you don't know what you want, need, and desire, then invest the time to figure it out.

When it comes to your partner, don't forget that they can't read your mind. No matter how much you wish they could, it's not going to happen. Be realistic and speak up for your needs in a respectable and assertive manner. Dysfunction attracts dysfunction, so you owe it to yourself to get healthy as soon as possible.

HOMEWORK

Set your balanced-life intentions. Think of your need to find balance toward a healthier self as a circle. Each area that needs to be improved is a part of the circle. When one part is removed, the whole circle becomes un-balanced. Then you're not rolling well, and life becomes more difficult. The ultimate goal is to stay balanced more often than not. Stop worrying that you have to keep everything perfectly balanced all the time, because that's impossible. For each area below, start by creating two goals you are willing to commit to. For now, start with two goals for each, then add additional ones in the future. What are two goals you can identify to help you have more balance in your life?

- Physical self
- Emotional self
- Sexual self
- Spiritual self
- Social self
- Work/career self
- Personal self
- Hobbies/interests

TIP 11:
IMPROVE YOUR SELF-IMAGE

One of the most important contributors of happiness in life is how you see yourself. How you view yourself both internally and externally directly correlates with how healthy you are as an individual. It would be nice if we were all born with healthy self-esteem, but that isn't the world we live in. We have to work to improve how we see ourselves.

It is a huge turnoff to everyone around you if you don't like who you are. Whether it's in a relationship or friendship, a negative self-image is unattractive. Commit to improve how you see yourself on a daily basis.

DON'T BE A DEBBIE DOWNER

Think of someone you know who constantly puts themselves down. You may see them as a Debbie Downer because they constantly talk about what they don't like about themselves. They may say they are too fat, not pretty, or that they don't deserve happiness. They often ruin the mood with their negativity.

Do you enjoy being around this kind of person? Maybe you end up telling them how great they are in an attempt to help them see their positive qualities. Maybe you try changing the subject to get them to not be so negative. It can be exhausting to be around someone who is negative about themselves so often.

Don't be this kind of person. You have control over this and have worked too hard to improve your life. This doesn't mean you have to see yourself in a beautiful light all the time, which impossible for anyone unless they're a narcissist. I'm asking you to have a better view of yourself just 50 percent of the time. It may be difficult at first, but with practice, you can do it.

IT'S NEVER TOO LATE

It doesn't matter how old you are or what you thought of yourself in the past, it's never too late to get serious about improving your self-image. What matters is what you're willing to do now, in this moment, to improve the way you see yourself. Again, we're not expecting perfection here—just forward movement in your goals.

The image you have of yourself doesn't have to be perfect all the time, but you do deserve to see the positives about yourself on a regular basis. The good news is that you're the only one who can make it happen and that with a bit of work, it's entirely possible.

Start by focusing on your strengths. And give yourself permission to invest time, effort, and energy into working on you. If you do, it will be impossible for you to not see positive things about yourself. Even if it's just a few things, at least it's something.

HOMEWORK

1. For the next seventy-two hours, whenever you look into a mirror, try looking deep into your eyes. Say something you like about yourself, either outwardly or inwardly. This exercise works best if you look *deep* into your eyes. See how many opportunities you can find to really look at yourself. Be gentle with yourself, refusing to focus on any negative traits you feel you have, and strive to see the beauty that is in you. Here are a few examples of what you can say to yourself to improve your self-image: "I am a strong person." "I deserve to be happy." "I like how my skin looks today." "I don't have to be perfect." "I am starting to like what I see."

TIP 12:
KNOW YOUR FINANCES AND BE INDEPENDENT

Finances can make or break a relationship. Money doesn't have to make your world go around, but it does affect how you connect with your partner.

If you spend excessively, don't pay bills on time, and don't plan for the future, you are failing in your half of the relationship. It is important to understand and manage your finances. Doing so leaves you feeling confident, competent, and in control. Ask anyone who they would find more attractive—someone who understands their finances or someone who is clueless when it comes to managing money. Keep in mind this has nothing to do with the amount of money you have.

WHICH TYPE OF PERSON WOULD YOU CHOOSE?

If you had to decide between a relationship with someone who is irresponsible with money or someone who is in control of their finances, which would you choose? If you choose the person who is in control of their finances, you owe it to yourself and your relationship to be this type of person.

Don't use the excuse that you have zero money or savings. The concept of financial independence and being competent has nothing to do with the amount of money you have.

IT'S TIME TO GET REAL

If you want to invest in a healthy relationship, you need to embrace your independence and your responsibility for the state of your finances. Learn how to balance your bank statement, create a monthly budget, pay your bills on time, and start a savings account. Don't use the excuse that you were not taught how to do this. There are great books and websites where you can learn these skills.

Don't lie to yourself by thinking you can take control of your money at some future date. Denial will prevent you from accomplishing your monetary goals. There's no better time to start managing your money more wisely than now.

Since it can be overwhelming to think about managing your money or not having any money to manage, begin with small steps, such as making a list of the things you need to do to get your finances under control.

Have you done the following?

- I know how to and manage my bank statement monthly.
- I have a list of my monthly bills.
- I have a savings account.
- I have started saving money for retirement.
- I have a monthly budget I use to manage bills.

Begin with the simplest task on the list above—writing down all your bills each month, including due dates, amounts due, and percentage rates (if applicable). Then move to the next task, until you've completed each item on the list.

FREE YOURSELF

Awareness and insight on your ability to manage your finances will provide you with a sense of freedom. This doesn't mean that you will be debt free, because you will still have bills to pay, but having a financial plan will give you peace and confidence. When you have a better understanding your finances, you gain freedom and positively affect your relationship with your partner.

Don't be afraid of your finances. Deal with your fears and stop avoiding improvement in this area. Your financial situation will not change until you learn how to manage it.

It doesn't matter if you are single, married, or in a relationship, you have to start now if you want to be in control of your finances. It doesn't matter if you were not taught how to do this when you were younger. You are an adult now. The time for denial is over. It's time to figure out how to better manage your finances.

HOMEWORK

Answer the following questions about your current financial status.

1. Do you know how much money you spend on fixed and variable expenses each month?

2. Do you know how much money you bring home after taxes each month?

3. Do you have a spreadsheet of your monthly bills, balances due, and interest you pay?

4. Do you have a 401k or retirement plan you invest in monthly?

5. Do you have a savings account you put money into each month?

If you answered no to any of these questions, you need to find the answers today. Don't use the excuse that you're not good with money. The days of avoidance are over; it's time to get to work on improving this area of your life.

You don't have to be good with money to get your financial status in check. All you need is a plan. There are many free templates, programs, and ideas online. And if you have a friend who's great at managing their finances, ask them for help.

Don't feel ashamed or embarrassed asking for a few tips. Do what it takes to build your confidence in this area. The shame and embarrassment come when your financial failings ruin your relationship.

TIP 13:
REMAIN AN INDIVIDUAL
WITHIN THE COUPLE

The definition of a healthy couple is two individuals who are healthy and balanced more often than not. This means both people in the relationship need to be their healthiest selves. As we've been stressing, the good news is that you are only responsible for you. However, you will suffer if you are in a relationship with someone who is not responsible for themselves. If your partner decides to not make their own self-improvements, you will be negatively affected.

WHEN THE NEW WEARS OFF

Most individuals are independent before they meet their partner. Then the couple begins to spend all their time together at this early stage of the relationship. As time passes and the feelings of the new relationship experience (NRE) wear off, many have lost their identity.

They have spent less time with their friends and doing things they used to enjoy and often lose touch with the things that are important to them because of their involvement in the relationship. Some even begin to develop codependent tendencies and are unable to see themselves as an individual separate from the couple. This can be dangerous and unhealthy for the relationship.

DON'T BE CODEPENDENT

Do you have a difficult time being alone in the relationship? Are you unhappy if your partner goes out with friends or spends time doing things outside the relationship, such as personal interests or hobbies.

If so, you'll find you're much happier if you learn that it's okay to be alone in the relationship. This isn't the same as being disconnected from your partner, where you both aren't fully present in the relationship.

Being "alone" means being an individual and not feeling like you have to be with your partner all the time. Your partner needs time and space for separate interests and friends. This not only gives them freedom but also sets you free to pursue your own interests.

And as you allow your partner the space to be who they are, you are fostering trust within the relationship. The expectation that the couple needs to be together continually can be suffocating and cause you to lose yourself in the relationship. Giving one another space will only help the relationship improve. If you are unsure whether this applies to you, consider these examples:

- You get upset if your partner goes out to dinner with their friends.
- You don't want your partner to go to the gym unless you go with them.
- You don't have any personal hobbies or interests you enjoy, so you don't understand why they have them.

If any of this sounds familiar, you have some work to do. Rather than feel overwhelmed or upset that this is an issue for you, accept that this is an area you can improve in.

YOU ARE MORE THAN JUST YOUR RELATIONSHIP

It's important that each of you has individual interests, hobbies, and friends outside the relationship. You both need space, time with friends, and time to be alone so you can continue to grow individually. Then you can really enjoy and appreciate the quality time you get to spend together.

If you feel jealous, concerned, or have a hard time with your partner doing things without you, you need to assess your relationship.

Start by asking yourself the following questions:

- Is there a reason I feel this way?
- How long have I felt this way?
- How is it impacting my relationship?

This has nothing to do with love or concern for your partner. It could be a red flag that you are dependent or codependent on your partner. As mentioned, being codependent is unattractive. If someone does find it attractive, please see this as a red flag.

Your happiness depends on your ability to improve in this area of your life. You deserve happiness, which involves a balance between being an individual and being a couple. Plan to visit a friend, join a meet-up group, start an art project, or engage in whatever interests you have. Just do something that makes you happy.

You are unique. There is no one on this planet quite like you. Enjoy exploring what makes you, you. Find out what makes you the amazing person you are.

A healthy couple allows and celebrates each other's individuality. Remember, you want someone to be *in* your life, not *be* your life.

HOMEWORK

Answer the following questions:

1. Have you lost yourself in your relationship? If you answered yes, what does being lost mean to you?

2. Do you have a difficult time remembering yourself as an individual?

3. What activities, hobbies, and interests were important to you before you started dating your partner?

4. What did you do that allowed these activities to change or stop?

5. What do you need to do to get back to being a healthy individual?

TIP 14:
KNOW WHEN TO USE
LOGIC VERSUS EMOTION

You make many decisions every day, some requiring more thought than others. From work, to family, to relationships, to friendships, you may feel like you don't have space to make a bad decision. I want you to think about the last important decision you made. Think about the process of making that decision.

Ask yourself these three questions:

- Did I make my decision based on emotion or logic?
- When making the decision, did I create a pros/cons list?
- Did I talk with someone who would be direct with me?

THE DANGER OF EMOTIONAL DECISIONS

There aren't many good decisions made when based on emotion. Often, when we make bad decisions, we don't engage in logical thinking.

Because making decisions based on emotion can ruin relationships, it's important to stop and think before you act. You will always get a better outcome using a logical approach versus a frantic, emotional response.

If you feel you need to respond emotionally to get your partner's attention, you've got some issues you need to deal with. Talk with your partner about these concerns so you can work together to problem solve.

For example, professional boxers don't fight with emotion; they fight with logic and strategy. They plan ahead with their team and study their competitor's previous fights. They develop a game plan. This doesn't mean they don't have emotion. Boxers do show their emotions; however, it is logic and strategy that helps them win the fight. If the boxer enters the ring and uses more emotion than logic, they will lose.

EXAMPLES OF EMOTIONAL DECISIONS

We often do whatever it takes to feel better in the moment. We want to feel good and know that if we _____, (insert any emotional decision) we will feel better.

Here are a few examples of what an emotional decision looks like. If these don't sound familiar, think of the last emotional decision you made.

- You know you will feel better if you buy that purse, even when you know you can't afford it. So you act on your emotions instead of thinking rationally. But the rush of endorphins is fleeting, and you're left with the reality that you can't pay your bills because you splurged on a purse.
- You think you will feel better by texting or cyberstalking your ex-partner. It's only a message, and no one has to know. This decision is based on emotion, not logic. Logic would tell you that it isn't

a good idea and will only backfire. However, you choose to ignore logic and send the message.

My clients often say, "My head is telling me one thing, but my heart is telling me something different." My response is always the same: "Which will result in more hurt—what your head is telling you or your heart?" The answer is always the heart because it's based on emotion and love.

That's because you want to feel good and stimulate your pleasure-seeking center. You want to avoid pain. You're often willing to make a bad decision based on emotion in order to feel good regardless of how short-lived it is. Again, there are few good decisions made when based on emotions.

DIFFERENCES IN MEN AND WOMEN

Whereas men typically use logic and problem-solving when making decisions, women typically come from an emotional place. This is one of the reasons men and women struggle to understand each other.

Men often approach things from a linear perspective—they understand best when one thing leads to another, then another. They see things as straight and linear. Women usually approach things through going forward and backward without a linear pattern. This is why men often think women are all over the place when they try to make a decision. Men see things as matter-of-fact, while women are more abstract with how they view things.

This is why women need to vent and talk things out in order to problem solve, which is different from men, who typically only ask questions and extract information in order to problem solve.

This does not mean men don't make emotional decisions, but how they process information is different than how women do.

It's important you see how your partner uses logic versus emotion. Also, be sure to share with them how you have evolved in your ability to use logic versus emotion. Let this discussion be an opportunity to connect more intimately as you come to better understand one another.

TRY AND PREVENT HEARTACHE

If your goal is to avoid getting your heart broken, you will need to listen to your head versus your heart. The worst feeling is looking back at an emotional decision and admit that you knew better but did it anyway.

No one can make the right decisions all the time. The goal is to develop a process for making decisions in a logical, healthy way.

HOMEWORK

Answer the following questions:

1. Do you listen more to your emotional side or your logical side when making decisions?

2. Do you want to change how you make decisions? If so, what are you willing to do differently in your decision-making process?

3. What barriers do you face in changing how you make decisions?

4. Identify one person you know who makes good decisions. What is it about this person that leads them to make good decisions?

5. List three strengths you have that will help you make better decisions.

TIP 15:
STOP PUTTING YOUR PARTNER LAST

If your partner has become your last priority, you are actively contributing to the end of your relationship. You may not even realize you're doing this. Think back over the past few weeks. How much quality time, connection, and affection have you given your partner? If you have a difficult time remembering, you need to take action today. It's vital to find ways to connect every day.

Don't feel like there's enough time in a day? Not an excuse. It's time you put your partner first. If you don't, you may lose them or ruin your relationship.

You may feel like you didn't plan for this to happen and that you're not actively trying to hurt your relationship. Regardless, now that you are aware of it, you have to hold yourself accountable. Don't wait for your partner to hold you accountable.

MAKING EXCUSES

If you find yourself justifying your behavior or making excuses, at least be honest about it. Here are a few common excuses we often use to justify why we put our partner last.

- I'm waiting for the kids get older. Then I'll focus on our relationship.
- I work all day, take care of the kids, and don't have any energy for anyone else.
- My partner doesn't make me his priority, so why should I make him mine?
- There will be time for us as a couple when the kids go to college.

If you've already been thinking your relationship will end soon, it would make sense that you aren't prioritizing your partner. However, you have to be able to live with your behaviors and actions, so be the bigger person and do the next right thing.

If neither of you prioritized the other, you've probably built resentments and feel contempt toward one another. Resentment is anger that has turned inward and causes you to be unhealthy. It multiplies and surfaces when arguments arise, which leads you to pull further away from your partner.

THE RESULT OF PUTTING YOUR PARTNER LAST

Mike and Pam came to me a few years back because they loved one another but were struggling with anger and resentment. Mike was frustrated because Pam put everyone else's needs before his. He told me he felt lonely and wanted his wife back. Pam explained she was a busy working mom and it was hard to balance everything.

After the third session, Mike told her he felt she purposely took on responsibilities and activities to avoid spending time with him. Through their work, Pam was able to tell Mike she felt resentful of his job, which included travel. She felt he got to escape home and stress when he traveled with work.

She resented having to work full-time and care for their two children without his help. She finally admitted she *was* finding reasons and excuses that took her away from him, though she didn't fully realize she was doing this until she said it out loud.

Thankfully, Mike and Pam were able to work through their anger and resentment and heal their relationship. The turning point came when Pam heard Mike tell her he valued her and wanted her to value him as well. Pam was able to heal her resentment and change her behavior, which included making time for Mike when he was home.

She was also able to create a new schedule that allowed her time alone while Mike watched the children. Once Pam identified her need to balance the different areas of her life, her stress lessened dramatically and their marriage improved. Happily, her decision to stop putting Mike last led her to get her own needs met.

IF THEY ARE PUTTING YOU LAST

If your partner is putting you last, remember—you can't change them regardless of how hard you try. You can tell them how you feel and that you would like them to make more of an effort, but to see change, you have to create change in yourself. Worst case, you get healthy, which leads you to make better decisions about the future of your relationship. Best case, you both change in a positive direction, and the relationship moves to a healthier place.

This gives you the opportunity to view your relationship from a different perspective and keeps you motivated to make positive changes. As for the fate of the relationship, that's for you to decide, but you have to be healthier so you can make the best decisions for you, not your partner.

HOMEWORK

1. Relationship timeline. You will need a sheet of paper and pencil. Start by drawing a horizontal line across the page. This will be the timeline for your relationship.

   - On the far left side, mark the year or month your relationship started.
   - On the far right, mark the current year.
   - Mark the year or month the relationship was at its best and write *best*.
   - Mark the year or month the relationship was at its worst and write *worst*.
   - Mark the year or month you stopped making your partner your priority.
   - Mark the year or month your partner stopped making you a priority.
   - Mark major life events that impacted the relationship.

2. As you look back at the timeline, do you see any patterns?

3. Can you identify when your feelings about your relationship and your partner changed? What was happening in your life at that time?

TIP 16:
DEAL WITH AND HEAL
RESENTMENTS

One way to ruin a relationship is to think that it's about you all of the time. This includes your pain, sadness, and feelings of being a victim. This has to change if you want your relationship to improve. Don't find an excuse to blame, react, or act like a victim when things don't go the way you would like them to.

A relationship is made up of two people, so be sure you look at what *you*, not your partner, are responsible for. Don't automatically fall into the victim role. If you do, you will have an unhealthy relationship.

RESENTMENT CAN DESTROY A RELATIONSHIP

Feelings of resentment can destroy a relationship. Even though your partner may not realize you feel this way, they can sense it in your behavior. When you slam the door as you leave, roll your eyes when they talk, or dismiss them, you are showing passive-aggressive behavior—a behavior that destroys connection.

Resentment does not disappear on its own. You will need to commit to doing the work of healing your resentment. Your relationship depends on your ability to work through it as a couple

Resentment will prevent you from being intimately connected. This is one of the major reasons a couple will have a hard time working through problems. When a couple can't separate their current argument from the resentment underneath the issue, and when issues are left unsettled, unresolved, or are ignored, they can easily turn into resentments.

For example, you ask your partner to help prepare dinner. They to tell you they will help you but never do. Your frustration and anger regarding their lack of follow-through builds, and you begin to think of other areas in the relationship they don't follow up on. You also compare it to all the things you do for them on a daily basis.

Then comes the day you stop talking to them because they don't seem to listen anyway. You push them away even when they try to connect with you, your resentment keeping you disconnected.

Resentment can't be ignored or denied. It has to be brought to light and healed or a couple can't move forward.

HOW TO DEAL

If you want to heal the resentment you have toward your partner, you'll need to identify, work through, and find acceptance with the problems of the past. If resentment is anger turned inward, ask yourself what led to the anger. Then, from a logical perspective, ask yourself if you played a role in this. It's hard to look inward and question your own culpability, especially if you feel hurt, but there's no short cut here. You have to go through this to get to other side, where you'll find healing.

Remember, you are responsible only for healing *your* resentments. Your partner is responsible for healing theirs. It will take both of you being committed to the process of repair.

HOMEWORK

Answer the following questions and complete the exercises to help you heal your resentments.

1. Make a list of your resentments you have about your partner. Write them out in detail.

2. Looking at your resentment list, are there any you can begin to let go of and find freedom from? If so, put a line through them.

3. Identify what role you may have played in each of these resentments. Really push yourself to take accountability for your part. Write out what role you played in each of them. Resentment building takes two people, and I want to challenge you to see your part in the process.

4. Identify the right time to talk with your partner about your list. Be sure to share what you learned about yourself through the process. Make sure you give your partner a chance to share their perspective as well.

5. Are you feeling brave? Ask your partner to make their own resentment list.

TIP 17:
LOVE AS AN ADJECTIVE
VERSUS A VERB

One of the most common phrases I hear as a therapist is "If he loved me, he would _____." You can fill the blank with almost anything. Despite the fantasies we have about it, the *idea* of being in love isn't enough to keep a relationship healthy. Love is an action, and without action, a relationship won't survive.

DON'T LET LOVE CONFUSE YOU

It's easy for women to confuse the meaning of the word *love*. They mistakenly associate the idea of love with a fantasy, a romantic movie, or a love song. These things have a way of influencing what we expect and hope for when it comes to love.

Remember what you thought love and a relationship would look like when you were younger? Did you think you would follow a certain timeline or have a set of expectations? Did you think you would fall in love, date for a specific amount of time, get engaged, have your dream wedding, have children, and grow old together?

Did this dream come true for you? Are you blissfully happy because your relationship timeline happened the way it did? If so, good for you. That is something to celebrate. For the majority of women, this isn't the case. There is a huge difference in how they imagined their relationship and the reality of what is. Often, life doesn't turn out how we expect it to, and not all relationships last, regardless of how much love we have.

But you are not doomed to a lifetime of unhappiness. You are not out of luck or stuck in your current circumstance. You are the master of your future. You have the right to go or stay in any relationship and the ability to change things in your life.

YOU CAN'T TURN IT OFF AND ON

Women often view love as something they can turn on or off depending on what their partner does. When a relationship falls apart, we probably still have some level of love for our partner.

Imagine how great it would be if once a relationship ended we could just flip a switch and were no longer in love? Getting over a breakup would be so much easier.

Avoid having a false reality of what love "should" look like. Don't fall into the trap of comparing your relationship to someone else's. You don't know what goes on behind closed doors.

The reality is that love sometimes looks different than we thought it would. It also looks different than how we would like it to. It's a good thing we have the ability to navigate where we want to go in life. We also have the right and permission to change our mind at any time about the future of the relationship.

ACTION VERSUS ADJECTIVE

Let's break down the difference of love as an adjective versus love as a verb. An adjective describes, identifies, or quantifies something. A verb signifies action. Many think of love as a feeling or a description of a feeling.

If your partner cheats on you, they may say "I never stopped loving you." However, they did STOP showing the ACTION of love. When they cheated on you, they stopped acting in love.

I'm not trying to sugarcoat infidelity or make it seem less serious. I want you to think of the difference in the *idea* of loving someone versus loving someone through your actions. Heartbreak is a horrible thing that takes a long time to heal from, and there are couples who may never heal from it.

I want you to understand the need for love to be an action. You need to show love through action, and you need to see love in action from your partner. Words don't have much meaning without action. If you settle for words without actions, you are showing your partner what you are willing to put up with.

WORDS AREN'T ENOUGH

Why stay in a relationship with someone who tells you what you want to hear in the moment but never backs it up with action? Empty words and promises will leave you feeling incomplete. Don't accept words when you deserve actions. And don't give words when you need to be showing action.

If there are issues of trust within the relationship, the only two things that can repair those issues are doing the next right thing and giving yourselves time to heal. Don't put too much pressure on yourself. You don't have to decide right now, in the moment, what you will do. You can take as much time as you need. You are the one making the final decision, and you have to live with it, so make it using logic, not emotion.

HOMEWORK

Answer the following questions about your view of love and whether that view has changed over the years.

1. When you were a teenager, how did you define and view love?

2. As an adult, how do you define and view love?

3. Is there any difference in how you defined love when you were younger versus now? What is interesting to you about these differences?

4. What experiences have led you to see changes in your definition and view of love?

5. How often have you settled for words rather than actions in your relationships?

6. How can you change to ensure you receive the action of love instead of the idea of love?

TIP 18:
YOU WILL NEVER BE LOVED EXACTLY HOW YOU WANT TO BE

In the spirit of fixing yourself as opposed to trying to fix your partner, please realize that you will never be loved exactly how you want to be. This may seem like a negative way of looking at things, but it is realistic. Love will not look the way you thought it would. It may have some semblance of what you hoped for, but odds are it looks completely different than what you expected.

HOW DID YOU IMAGINE LOVE TO BE?

When you were growing up, what did you imagine love would look like? Was it someone who made a lot of money, had a dream job, played in a band, never hurt you, or brought you flowers when you had a bad day?

In reality, love looks more like a partner who thinks to ask you on their way home from work if you need anything from the grocery store. This isn't dreamy, but small acts of kindness are a reflection of your partner's love for you. If they pick up flowers for you while they are at the store, that's a huge bonus.

Though you may have a list of expectations you feel your partner "should" be meeting, it's likely this list is unrealistic and impossible to achieve. If you expect that a person can love you exactly how you want to be loved, you're going to be disappointed.

There isn't a person who can be everything to you all the time. It is impossible for one person to meet all the needs you require to be whole. This is a work you have to do for yourself. If you have a partner who is healthy and well balanced, consider yourself fortunate.

BEING WANTED VERSUS BEING NEEDED

Typically, men would rather be wanted than needed, while most women would rather be needed than wanted. When women feel needed or valued, they feel secure within their relationship.

The need for men to be desired is rooted in their physical makeup. It's important for women to be aware of this trait, because those who aren't often find themselves with unhealthy partners. Then they can't figure out how they ended up in toxic relationships.

Lee and Cindy are a great example of this. Lee has an endless list of needs, and Cindy likes to feel needed. Thought she gets her self-esteem stroked by taking care Lee, she sometimes struggles with it. But it isn't Lee's fault if Cindy doesn't say no or speak up for her needs,

Cindy has to fix herself by making changes and exploring what her actual needs are. It is her responsibility to discuss them with Lee so that he understands them. She also needs to resolve her desire to be "needed" in an unhealthy way.

OUR IMAGINATION IS RESPONSIBLE FOR LOVE

One of my favorite quotes by Marcel Proust is, "It is our imagination that is responsible for love, not the other person." If this is true, the idea of how we see love comes from within and not from someone else.

This means that how we imagine love determines how we create love and that it has little to do with our partner. Be sure to take a few minutes and reflect on this within your current or past relationship. You may gain new insight into what you want love to actually look like in your life.

HOMEWORK

1. What are your expectations for your partner?

2. Are any of your expectations unrealistic? Can you change any of your expectations to be more realistic?

3. What wishes/dreams/fantasies of your partner are you holding on to?

4. Is it possible to let go of those wishes/dreams/fantasies to allow a healthy relationship to grow? If not, you may want to revisit your relationship and make other plans.

TIP 19:
CHANGE YOUR UNREALISTIC EXPECTATIONS

Do you have unrealistic expectations of yourself or your partner? It's important to be aware if you do because these types of expectations can lead to continual disappointment and keep you from achieving the kind of relationship you both deserve.

YOUR PERFECTIONISM IS HURTING YOU

While perfectionistic thinking can be a strength, it can also be a downfall. This type of thinking often causes you to feel dissatisfied with your results. And so you work harder, but you're never happy. You often are not able to attain your goal because you are never good enough.

Perfectionist thinking leads to unrealistic expectations and to disappointment. Look at the goals you've set for yourself or the things you expect to accomplish. How realistic are they, and what time frame do you expect to complete them in? When you don't accomplish them, are you hard on yourself? Even when you almost reach your goals, do you feel that since you didn't reach them, you don't deserve any credit? If you find that you continually beat yourself up for not accomplishing your goals, it could be that your goals are unrealistic.

It's often the case that when we set unrealistic expectations for ourselves, we also set them for our partner. For example, if you complain your partner doesn't pick up after themselves or they never help out with chores, you may have unrealistic expectations.

It's okay to ask your partner for help, but don't expect them to do things the way you think they should. Don't complain about how they did a chore; just be grateful they did it.

I often hear women complain that their partner doesn't pick up after themselves or help around the house. The partner often explains that they do clean up after themselves, but it isn't to the standard she is looking for and she goes behind them to redo the chore. It doesn't matter if they clean or not, it's never enough. If your partner doesn't feel like they can win either way, they will not feel motivated to help next time.

It would be unrealistic for your partner to do everything you want them to do exactly the way you think they should. You are two different people with different ways of doing things. This is where you need to practice acceptance and gratitude. When you show gratitude for their help with the chores and give them positive reinforcement, they'll be more likely to help out again in the future. Also, don't go behind them and redo. Simply be glad that the chore is completed.

DON'T BE A NAG

One of the worst things you can do is nag or chastise your partner. It doesn't matter how frustrated or aggravated you are because they don't follow through. Another common complaint I hear during couples counseling is that one partner feels that the other wont' stop pushing them to do a task. Instead of a nag, be a problem solver by focusing on what you can change to help you feel better about the situation.

Expecting them to stack the dishes in the dishwasher the way you do is unrealistic and will leave you feeling disappointed, angry, and frustrated. It doesn't matter if your way of doing it makes the most sense. Let go of your pride. If you want the relationship to work, let go of that unrealistic expectation or do the dishes yourself.

The other option is to feel you are right all of the time, remain frustrated, and cause conflict within the relationship. The choice is yours. It depends on the type of relationship you want. Learn to let go, accept their way of doing things, or do it yourself.

HOMEWORK

1. Make a list of the expectations you have for your partner. Don't hold back, regardless of how unrealistic they are.

2. After you have made your list, take a separate sheet of paper and draw two columns, then label them *realistic* and *unrealistic*. Now, take your list of expectations and put each under one of the two columns. If an expectation is realistic, write it under the *realistic* column. If it is unrealistic, write it under the *unrealistic* column.

3. Once you have completed your *realistic* and *unrealistic* list, see if you can challenge your unrealistic expectations to make them more realistic. You may be able to move a few to the other column. But for those you are unable change, draw a line through them and begin to practice the art of letting go. Holding on to unrealistic expectations only leads to more disappointment.

TIP 20:
ACCEPT THAT THE RELATIONSHIP LOOKS DIFFERENT

Have you ever wondered why your partner doesn't see the relationship the same way you do? Have you ever gotten frustrated because of it?

It's unrealistic and irrational to think your partner will see your relationship through your eyes, because you are two very different people. It is impossible for two people to view the relationship the same way all the time. You each have different priorities, roles, and needs within the relationship.

THINGS YOU NEED TO DEFINE

While it is common to view the relationship differently, it's important to make sure you both have a clear understanding of what the relationship is. This can also change as the relationship continues through the years.

To ensure that you are both on the same page, try discussing how you each define the following:

- Love
- Trust
- Sex
- Intimacy
- Cheating/affair/infidelity

The ideal situation is to have this discussion when you first start dating. However, we will assume you didn't discuss these things. The good news is, it's never too late. It may surprise you just how differently your partner defines and perceives things. For example, I worked with a couple who defined cheating very differently. The husband viewed cheating as having sex with another woman and thought he wasn't cheating if there wasn't physical interaction. The wife considered it cheating if a woman reached out to him and he didn't share it with her.

Many women don't realize how important it is to discuss their future goals with a partner before marriage. So many problems can prevented if these things are taken care of. Here are a few discussions that need to happen when you begin to date someone.

- Do you want children?
- Is religion or a spirituality important to you?
- If we have children, do you want them to be raised with certain religious beliefs?
- Who will be the primary caretaker of the children, and who will continue to work?
- What are your career goals?

- What are your financial goals?
- What are you planning for retirement?
- What is your financial status? How do you view spending, saving, and budgeting?

You may have an expectation of what the relationship will look like in the future. The problem is that your partner may see it differently. This is why it is crucial for you to discuss the future with your partner.

FINDING EQUALITY WITHIN THE RELATIONSHIP

If you feel uneasy, uncomfortable, or that something's just not right within the relationship, be sure to address it. Don't ignore it and think it will just go away. That's highly unlikely. Many times, this discomfort is due to an unequal balance within the relationship.

If a relationship becomes unbalanced, it feels unfair to one or both people. The more equal the relationship, the more respect both people feel for one another. Here are a few things that can lead to the feeling of inequality within the relationship.

- Infidelity/cheating
- Addiction
- Housework/chores/home responsibilities
- Parenting styles
- Medical conditions
- Stay at home versus work outside the home
- Job loss
- High earner versus low earner
- Finances

These issues can also affect trust and intimacy. When one person loses trust in how their partner addresses any of these issues, it can cause a decrease in intimacy or the feeling of connection. Make sure you are addressing these issues in a healthy way.

YOU BOND DIFFERENTLY

Another way a relationship may look different than you expected is in how the two of you bond. Typically, men (and some women) bond through experiences. This means they connect through doing an activity. For example, two men can watch a football game and barely talk to one another. Every now and then they may make a comment about the game. However, they are perfectly content watching the game together using few words and consider it bonding.

This is different than for most women (and some men), who connect through talking or venting. Can you imagine two women watching a football game and barely saying anything? I love football and often talk through the entire game, either about my sometimes not-so-nice thoughts on how they are playing or about something totally unrelated to the game.

On average, women speak many more words per day than men do. This is because women process what they are experiencing through talking. As mentioned previously most men speak in order to problem solve.

It can be a problem for women who want to talk when their partner doesn't understand that this is how they process and connect. Take David and Leah. They have been dating for years. David has been trying to get Leah to go to a concert with him. Leah is angry at David because he isn't open to the idea of moving across town. Leah doesn't want to go with him because she is irritated and doesn't feel he takes her wishes into consideration.

The best way to work this out is for Leah to agree to go to the concert with David if he is willing to listen and discuss her reasons for wanting to move. The relationship looks different than Leah thought it would because she didn't think she'd have to do things she didn't want to do to in order to get her needs met. She envisioned that David would always listen to her and consider her ideas.

HOMEWORK

1. What do you fantasize about your relationship or about your partner? How will your partner act, behave, and interact with you?

2. What is the reality? What does the relationship actually look like on a daily basis? How is the interaction between you and your partner?

3. Look back at your answers for 1 and 2. Compare these side by side. What do you notice? What feelings and thoughts do you have about them? What are the differences between how you both view them?

TIP 21:
LEARN ABOUT YOUR SEXUAL SELF

The top three issues that get couples into trouble are sex, finances, and communication. This tip focuses on learning more about your sexual self. Do not think you can pretend your sexual hang-ups are going to disappear. You have to deal with them, and it doesn't have to be scary, intimidating, or anxiety provoking.

It is a tremendous feat for the majority of women to acknowledge they even have a sexual side. The goal of finding comfort, respect, and peace with your sexual self is a struggle in our society, where women aren't supposed to discuss sex.

THERE IS NOTHING TO
BE EMBARRASSED ABOUT

What does it say about you if you discuss sex? Does it mean you are loose, or *that* kind of girl? Does it mean you don't have morals? We aren't encouraged to develop sexual self-esteem, but we are expected to have libidos and desires that match our partner's—which is completely unrealistic.

There is nothing to be ashamed of or embarrassed about when discussing sex. There is no need to worry about what someone will think. It's never too late to begin to have a healthy discussion about your sexual self. You deserve to feel pleasure.

How will you ever figure out your sexual self if you can't even talk about it? Begin by thinking about what feels good to you, not what feels good to your partner. Also, think about what doesn't feel good. Connect with your sexual self by having this internal discussion about your sexuality, needs, and desires.

If you feel uncomfortable thinking about these things, then take a deep breath and know you are normal. Many women have a hard time thinking about this topic. You have already done many hard things in your life. This is why you will be able to survive this exploration of your sexual self.

If you feel like you would rather avoid anything related to sex, please know that this is normal as well, especially as you get older. It doesn't mean anything is wrong with you or that you are broken. This is a good opportunity for you to explore how you view the role of sex. What purpose has it served in your life? What purpose does it serve now? If it doesn't serve a function, that can add to the reason you have seen a decline in your libido.

CHANGE FOR YOU, NOT THEM

Has your partner complained that you aren't sexual enough or that you never want sex? It is likely your partner views sex differently and feels that there isn't enough. This also becomes an issue when there are other problems within the relationship. Partners often see the roles of sex differently.

You are not expected to change for your partner. The goal is to make changes for your benefit. You don't have to become a sex machine, but if you want to feel more confident about yourself as a person, learning about your sexual self can be a huge benefit.

Be gentle with yourself. Give yourself permission to think about your sexuality and to have a healthy discussion with your partner. If you don't feel like your partner is open to discussing it, let them know of your concern. You deserve the time and space to figure out what you like and how you like it. Don't be silent and settle for a relationship where you're not treated as an equal. Speak up for what you like and don't like.

HOMEWORK

1. While growing up, what messages did you receive about sex?

2. How did these messages affect your sexual exploration?

3. What negative self-talk do you have concerning sex?

4. Does your partner desire sex more than you do?

5. If so, how does this make you feel, and does your partner know?

TIP 22: ACCEPT THAT YOU WILL VIEW SEX DIFFERENTLY

Has your partner or ex-partner ever complained about your lack of sexual desire? Is there a complaint that you either don't care enough about sex or are too focused on sex? Have you thought that something must be wrong with you sexually because of the affect it has on your relationship?

Every person views sex differently, and even at different parts of our lives our views vary. People use sex for many different reasons. It's not that one reason is more right than another; it's just different for everyone. It is very important that you identify how you view it and how your partner views it. This will help you better understand yourself and each other.

SEX MAY NOT BE THE ISSUE

Everyone wants to be desired at some point in their life. Think of the last time you really wanted your partner. If it has been awhile, are there are other areas of the relationship that need work?

Are there issues with communication? With trust? Is there conflict or disagreements turning you off? Have drugs or alcohol or a certain behavior interfered with the connection the two of you used to have?

Issues with intimacy are often secondary issues within the relationship. This is why you need to figure out the root cause of what's going on. It's likely not sex. The issue is what is getting in the way of sex.

THE HONEYMOON PHASE IS OVER

Remember when you first started dating and you couldn't keep your hands off each other? Was there a time when all you did was have sex and even skip events so you could be together? You did whatever you had to so that you could be with them.

Well, the honeymoon phase is officially over. It may have ended as early as six months, or it may have taken a few years. It has nothing to do with the couple being "happy" and everything to do with the new relationship wearing off and a long-term relationship setting in.

Children, financial stress, weight fluctuations, job stress, medication side effects, physical/mental illness, and infertility are just a few of the things that can take a hit on your intimacy. Sex can feel like a task or chore when you experience stress, changes in libido, or a loss of desire. This is normal. However, you have to be the one to decide whether you want to improve this area of the relationship.

DECIDE IF YOU WANT THINGS TO CHANGE

Your partner may feel rejected and start building resentments if you say no, just as you may feel hurt when your partner tells you no. It's important to see that you both have different sexual needs. There is nothing wrong with the relationship; it's just an opportunity for both of you to grow through this.

But in order to grow, you need to be able to talk about the difference in how you view sex and collaborate on how both of you can get your needs met. If you have worked on the other areas of your relationship, including communication, trust, and connection, you will be able to come to an agreement.

Staying in denial and pretending that intimacy isn't important will only create further damage. The goal is for you to trust one another enough to discuss intimacy and see it from one another's perspective.

FINAL THOUGHTS ABOUT SEX

There are a lot of things sex and intimacy can bring to a relationship, including fun, a feeling of connection, and an improved sense of trust. However, there are a few things sex cannot do:

1. Sex cannot fix a relationship. It can help two people grow closer and become more connected, but it isn't your main issue. Figure out the root cause of the relationship problem. When you do, and are able repair it, your intimacy will improve.
2. Sex does not equal love. Just because someone has sex with you does not mean they love you. It is a way some people show love, but don't think it's why they are having sex with you. This is a lesson many young women learn the hard way.
3. Don't use sex as a punishment or reward. This can cause conflict within a relationship. Holding back adds to the power struggle within the relationship and can cause resentment and frustration. Don't make a relationship harder than it has to be.

HOMEWORK

Everyone uses sex for different reasons. These reasons can also change as you grow older. If you can identify how you see the use of sex in your relationship, you can discuss it more freely with your partner. Here are a few uses to consider. Check the ones you identify with and share them with your partner.

_____ Sex as a fun activity

_____ Sex as punishment

_____ Sex as a form of togetherness

_____ Sex as proof

_____ Sex as a reward

_____ Sex as purely playful activity

_____ Sex as a way to communicate togetherness

_____ Sex as a mechanical duty

_____ Sex as an outlet for physiological or psychological tension

_____ Sex as an adventure

_____ Sex as a way to have babies

_____ Sex as a way of overcoming loneliness

TIP 23:
KNOW YOUR FEARS

Many of the behaviors that cause conflict in your relationship come from a place of fear. Do you become clingy when you feel your partner pulling away? Do you start pushing your partner away because you are scared of getting hurt? Ironically, these attempts to protect yourself end up hurting you because nothing in the relationship changes.

I challenge you to dig deep and explore what you are scared of. You are at a place in your life where you are capable of making changes. There's no better time. Life's not going to get easier, so peel back that layer of fear.

GET TO WORK

What are you afraid of? What are you worried about or scared will happen? Are your what-ifs leading you in circles? Are worry and anxiety causing issues within your relationship? If your inner narrative of questions is driving you crazy, change it.

You need to explore where your fear comes from and what it looks like. Identifying what the fear is all about will give you the greatest freedom, and you deserve freedom from chronic worry and fear. You deserve to live an authentic life where you don't have to hide from your fears. Your fear will only grow as big as you allow it to. You have the power to shrink and defeat it.

If you are in a relationship, you have a great advantage. A great way to build intimacy with your partner is to share these fears. Start by asking your partner to listen as you share what you are experiencing. Ask them to not interrupt you or try to problem solve, and explain that you just need them to listen. Tell them what you are fearful of and why it causes you to react in a negative way. Share with them anything they can do to help you work through your fear. Your partner can't read your mind and deserves to know what you are going through.

Allow yourself to be vulnerable, letting your walls down as your partner supports you. As you allow yourself to be vulnerable, you'll see growth and a better connection with your partner because you are showing them you trust them. Since trust and intimacy move in tandem, allowing yourself to be vulnerable automatically improves intimacy.

HOMEWORK

Answer the following questions to help you gain a better understanding of your fears.

1. My biggest worry is . . .

2. I fear that . . .

3. Past relationships have ended due to my fear of . . .

4. I have been told that I worry too much because I . . .

5. I would feel more comfortable sharing my fears if . . .

6. In my relationships with others, I fear that . . .

7. If I show someone I'm vulnerable, I fear that . . .

8. I don't like to share my fears with others because . . .

TIP 24:
STOP TESTING YOUR PARTNER

Do you wonder if your partner really cares about you but don't feel like you can discuss it openly with them? Have you ever tested your partner by asking questions or creating challenges to see if it will prove anything? What if you were able to talk to them about what you are feeling versus testing them?

Testing your partner sets them up for potential failure. It also shows your inability to express what you need. If you feel you have to test someone, you are trying to trick them. Obviously, this won't boost confidence and trust between the two of you. There is no benefit to telling your partner they have failed again.

THREATS DON'T WORK

I have worked with many women who make threats within their relationships. Making threats in a relationship doesn't solve any problems; in fact, threats actually hurt more than help. Threats are false promises you're not going to carry through with. If you were able to take action on your threats, you would have already done what you threatened to do.

If you threaten to leave your partner if they do X, and they actually do X and you don't leave, you are showing them how to treat you. Empty threats have no power. You teach others how you want to be treated by allowing or not allowing things to happen to you.

DO SOMETHING DIFFERENT

Why not try something different in your relationship? Why not step up and have the discussion you are avoiding?

There is no need for testing in a relationship. If you want to know the answer, ask. If you are afraid of the answer or want to continue avoiding issues, then keep testing. The choice is yours. Tests are for school, not relationships, so if you want to be an adult, act like one. The best approach if you want to see a change in your relationship is to change yourself.

HOMEWORK

1. What are you trying to find out by testing your partner?

2. What are you hoping they do when you test them?

3. Why is this important to you?

4. Have you tried talking to your partner about this?

5. What are the three things you can do to accomplish this goal?

TIP 25:
GET BACK TO BEING FRIENDS

The issues you may be struggling with in your relationship may have nothing to do with love. You can both love each other, but love isn't enough to create a healthy relationship. Most of the time, lack of love for one another isn't the issue.

I hear couples in strained relationships say that they love one another very much. They are often surprised when I tell them the problem is that they've stopped being friends with one another. They have stopped treating one another as they would a good friend and are taking one another for granted, often without even realizing it.

THE FRIENDSHIP SUFFERS

Life is so chaotic and busy there's often little time left for a couple. Work, children, family, medical issues, financial struggles, and many other demands on our time often take precedence, and the foundation of friendship we've established begins to erode.

Most couples make the mistake of putting their children before their relationship. When this happens, they end up feeling disconnected and robbing children of two connected parents. If you can't rekindle your friendship, there's little hope for your relationship.

The stark reality is that friendship is a necessity, not a luxury. Do you want to remain in a relationship with someone you don't treat as well as your friends? If you do want to work on the relationship, you have to start with friendship.

GET BACK TO THE BASICS

As you do the homework following this tip, you will be able to identify when the friendship started to fade. Start by challenging yourself to see things from your partner's perspective. Try to understand where they are coming from. Even if you don't agree with them, try to see the situation through their eyes.

This doesn't mean you're saying they are right. It simply means you're validating their feelings and their perspective. They want to know you are hearing what they have to say.

Your responsibility is to be a friend through the difficult issues that will certainly arise. There isn't room for resistance, stubbornness, or a need to be right. You wouldn't treat your best friend that way, so why is it okay to treat your partner that way? If you don't have some form of respect for your partner, your relationship will perish and you will have no one to blame but yourself.

HOMEWORK

1. Look back over your relationship timeline from tip 15 and identify when you stopped being friends. What was happening during your relationship at that time?

2. Did you realize that the relationship was changing?

3. Did you or your partner talk about these changes?

4. Did you or your partner attempt to work on your friendship?

5. If you could have done something different during that time, what would it have been? What would you have liked your partner to do?

6. Make a list of ten things that make your partner a good friend.

BONUS QUIZZES

DO YOU HAVE GOOD BOUNDARIES?

Do you have a difficult time establishing and maintaining boundaries? Use this quiz to determine if you have good boundaries.

YES **NO**

_____ _____ 1. I have a difficult time saying no to people.

_____ _____ 2. I have a hard time speaking up for what I need or want.

_____ _____ 3. I become frustrated when people ask something of me because I can't say no.

_____ _____ 4. I am a people pleaser.

_____ _____ 5. I like to make other people happy, even at my own expense.

_____ _____ 6. I often say yes to others when I want to say no.

_____ _____ 7. I give in to others even if I have said no earlier.

_____ _____ 8. I avoid conflict by going along with others, even when I don't want to. I will do anything to avoid conflict.

_____ _____ 9. I am often tired and exhausted because I take care of others and neglect myself.

_____ _____ 10. I like for others to make the decision or plans so I don't have to.

If you have:

- three or more checked *yes*, you need to work on standing up for yourself. You also need to create and establish healthy boundaries.
- four or more checked *yes*, you need to stop allowing others to dictate your behavior and actions. Your lack of boundaries is creating your unhappiness. No one can fix this but you.
- five or more checked *yes*, you need to have an honest conversation with yourself. It's time to create healthy boundaries if you want to find happiness.

DECIDING TO END A RELATIONSHIP?

Is your relationship on the rocks? Are you trying to decide to stay or go? Use this quiz to determine what's right for you.

YES   NO

_____ _____ 1. I am unhappy with my partner and the relationship more often than not.

_____ _____ 2. I can't remember the last time I enjoyed being around my partner.

_____ _____ 3. I realize I am in an unhealthy relationship.

_____ _____ 4. My family/friends are telling me I seem unhappy in my relationship.

_____ _____ 5. My relationship lacks intimacy and sex.

_____ _____ 6. My partner has an addiction that affects the relationship and my connection with them.

_____ _____ 7. I am in a codependent relationship.

_____ _____ 8. I have nothing in common with my partner.

_____ _____ 9. I dread being around my partner and avoid being at home with them.

_____ _____ 10. My partner is unwilling to work on our relationship issues.

If you have:

- three or more checked *yes*, you need to evaluate the benefit of remaining in the relationship. Does the good outweigh the bad? Is this relationship costing you more than it is benefiting you?

- four or more checked *yes*, these are red flags that your relationship is unhealthy. Take the steps to get healthy as an individual; this may mean ending the relationship.

- five or more checked *yes*, these are red flags that the relationship will not work. Stop trying to salvage an unhealthy relationship. Do what needs to be done to become your best self.

ARE YOU READY TO CHANGE YOUR LIFE?

Do you feel it's time for a change? Do you need the motivation to take the next step? Use this quiz to determine if you are ready to make real, lifelong changes.

YES   **NO**

_____ _____ 1. I am tired of doing the same things and getting the same results.

_____ _____ 2. I have tried in the past to make changes but could not follow through and hold myself accountable.

_____ _____ 3. I rarely feel motivated to make changes in my life.

_____ _____ 4. I rarely follow through with my goals.

_____ _____ 5. I could make the changes I want in my life if I had someone to help me.

_____ _____ 6. I often blame others for my issues.

_____ _____ 7. I know there is a better life than the one I'm living.

_____ _____ 8. My life is not where I thought it would be.

_____ _____ 9. I am willing to commit to making changes if someone will tell me what actions to take.

_____ _____ 10. I am dissatisfied with my life at this moment.

If you have:

- three or more checked *yes*, you know that making changes will help, but you may not be ready to take action.

- four or more checked *yes*, you know you need to make changes in certain areas of your life and are ready to take action. Start by surrounding yourself with a positive support system and people who want to see you succeed.

- five or more checked *yes*, you need to stop ignoring the universe, because it is telling you to make changes. Do not waste any more time. figure out the changes you need to make now. Your new life is right around the corner.

ABOUT THE AUTHOR

Dr. Kristie Overstreet is a clinical sexologist, psychotherapist, author, and relationship expert. She is also the author of *4 Weeks to Improve Your Relationship as a Couple*. Her upcoming book, *Finding Your True Self: A Guide to Gender Acceptance*, will be published in 2018. She has spent the past eleven years helping individuals, couples, and families become their best and is passionate about helping people improve their relationships.

Kristie is a sought-after expert in the areas of sex, relationships, and transgender identities. Her expertise has been featured on CNN and in *Self*, *Glamour*, *Cosmopolitan*, *Psychology Today*, *Woman's Day*, *Redbook*, *Readers Digest*, *Playboy*, and other media.

Printed in Poland
by Amazon Fulfillment
Poland Sp. z o.o., Wrocław

53080808R00068